3 -

D0394577

"Danae gives us sparkling, fresh insight into what really matters in life. Speaking with a wisdom beyond her years, she adds a charming touch of whimsy that makes this book a standout—like a sunflower in a summer garden!"

ROBIN JONES GUNN

Bestselling author of the Christy Miller series

"I'm so impressed with how God's wisdom radiates through Danae's writing in *Things I've Learned Lately.* While her essays primarily concern "ordinary" things, her message is anything but ordinary. I'm convinced her readers will be touched and challenged by this encouraging book. A great addition to any teen's library!"

MELODY CARLSON

Author of *Diary of a Teenage Girl* and *It's My Life*

"Seventeen-year-old Danae Jacobson captures the joys and challenges of her generation in a way that is sure to resonate with today's Christian teen. I highly recommend *Things I've Learned Lately* to any young person who wants to learn more about what matters most."

BRUCE WILKINSON

author of the *New York Times* bestsellers
The Prayer of Jabez and *Secrets of the Vine*

things
I've
learned
lately

DANAE
JACOBSON

Multnomah®Publishers *Sisters, Oregon*

Things I've Learned Lately
published by Multnomah Publishers, Inc.

© 2001 by Danae Jacobson
International Standard Book Number: 1-57673-951-1

Cover design by David Carlson Design
Cover image of house and dog by William Huber/Photonica
Cover image of shooting stars by Yutaka Iijima/Photonica
Cover image of teens by Eyewire
All other cover images by Photodisc

Scripture quotations are from:
The Holy Bible, New International Version
© 1973, 1984 by International Bible Society,
used by permission of Zondervan Publishing House

Multnomah is a trademark of Multnomah Publishers, Inc.,
and is registered in the U.S. Patent and Trademark Office.
The colophon is a trademark of Multnomah Publishers, Inc.

Printed in the United States of America

ALL RIGHTS RESERVED
No part of this publication may be reproduced, stored in a retrieval system,
or transmitted, in any form or by any means—electronic, mechanical,
photocopying, recording, or otherwise—without prior written permission.

For information:
MULTNOMAH PUBLISHERS, INC.
POST OFFICE BOX 1720
SISTERS, OREGON 97759

Library of Congress Cataloging-in-Publication Data

Jacobson, Danae.
  Things I've learned lately / by Danae Jacobson
    p. cm.
  ISBN 1-57673-951-1
  1. Teenage girls--Religious life. 2. Christian life. l. Title:
Things I have learned lately. II. Title.
  BV4551.3 .J33 2001
  242'.633--dc21

2001004676

02 03 04 05—10 9 8 7 6 5 4 3 2 1

For Avonléa, my beautiful, sweet cousin.

And for my Lord, my everything.

Contents

Acknowledgments 9

Introduction 13

Things I've Learned Lately 15

Chocolate Chip Cookies Taste Better As Dough 57

I'm Just Passing Through 59

You Don't Have to Know Your Future to Have One 63

Midnight Laughter Cleanses the Soul 67

It's Best to Believe the Best 71

A Good Book Is Really a Friend 75

It's Good to Do Nothing with God 79

Trying to Change a Friend Isn't Fair 81

It's a Morning Person's World 83

Coincidences Are Really "God Things" 87

A Friend Doesn't Have to Be Near to Be Close 91

"God Bless America" Is More than a Song 95

Romance Is Underrated 99

Love Slows Down to Really See 103

Ordinary Life Is a Beautiful Thing 105

Good Friends Aren't Afraid to Fight 109

Country Music Isn't So Bad after All 113

You Can Learn a Lot from Bad Teachers 117

Life Is Unfair, but God Is Good 121

Christmas Really Is about Gifts 125

Sometimes Others See Us Better than We See Ourselves 129

People Should Cry More Often 133

All Little Boys Miss Their Mommies at Bedtime 135

I'm Pretty As a Princess 139

Change Is Inevitable, but God Is Unchanging 143

I Don't Want to Be Religious 147

Memories Are a Treasure 149

People Are More Alike than Different 155

We Hear Best with Our Eyes 159

My Mom Understands 161

The Stars Shine Brighter When There Is No Moon 165

Pedestals Weren't Made for People 169

Children Know the Secret of Making Friends 173

Stereotypes Are Shortcuts 177

Love Has a Name 179

We Should Work at Liking Work 183

Three Little Words Can Set You Free 187

I'll Never Be Too Big for Hugs 191

The Hardest Person to Be Is Yourself 193

You Can't Get Close to Someone without Taking Risks 197

Life Is Short and Death Unthwartable 199

Passionate People Get More out of Life 205

There is a time for everything,

and a season for every activity under heaven:

a time to be born and a time to die,

a time to plant and a time to uproot,

a time to kill and a time to heal,

a time to tear down and a time to build,

a time to weep and a time to laugh,

a time to mourn and a time to dance,

a time to scatter stones and a time to gather them,

a time to embrace and a time to refrain,

a time to search and a time to give up,

a time to keep and a time to throw away,

a time to tear and a time to mend,

a time to be silent and a time to speak,

a time to love and a time to hate,

a time for war and a time for peace.

He has made everything beautiful in its time.

ECCLESIASTES 3:1-8, 11

Acknowledgments

First, foremost, and forever—thank You, Jesus, for loving me like You do, for being the perfect friend, and for always being faithful. I am Yours.

Also, thank you, Mrs. Weber, for everything. Without your guidance and challenges in English class, there would be no book. A good teacher *really* is a friend.

Thank you, Heather Kopp, for tackling and conquering the editing process with me. I learned so much from you, and I made a new friend in the process!

Thank you to my friends for being so excited for the book (more so than me sometimes!). Thanks for understanding when I was busy or distracted because of it. Thanks for letting me write about you and learn with you. You know who you are. You guys are the best friends I could ever ask for, and I would not be the same without each of you. You guys rock my world.

Thanks, **Sarah,** for typing this book for me; you saved my life. Sorry about the handwriting! Even more, thanks for being the dearest best friend ever.

Thank you to **everyone else** who knows me and still loves me! Thanks for all the encouragement. Thanks…

...**Bill Jensen,** for believing in my writing.

...**Robin Jones Gunn**—you are my inspiration.

...**Kelleigh** and **Lindsay**—I was more scared of you than of Multnomah if I didn't get the book done. ☺

...**Jim Gurney,** for all that words are not enough to explain.

...**Patti Ribb**—I love you so much. Thanks for letting God use you and for being there.

...**the Pederson Family,** for reading what I write—that encourages me so much!

...**to all the other amazing people** in my life that I haven't mentioned. I treasure each of you and your impact on this world and on me.

Finally, to **my family**—thanks for letting me write about you and for living with me.

Dad, thanks for believing I could do it and for encouraging me each step of this life. You know I am going to marry a guy like you.

Mom, thanks for helping type the book. But mostly thank you for being the kind of person, mother, and friend that you are. I am so glad I can call you my friend.

Blair, thanks for letting me skip out on some basketball games to write—I know I owe you big-time. I am so excited for the amazing guy God is making you into. I hope we can continue becoming friends.

Cammy, you are the sweetest sister ever. Your love for me blows me away, and I love seeing you learning to love like Jesus wants you to. You are beautiful and precious, to me and to Him. As you go through life and become a teenager, never forget that.

Cavan, I can't believe you are ten. No matter how old you get, you'll always be my "bug," okay? Don't let anyone take away your kindness, love, and sensitivity for others. I need to learn to be more like you in some of those areas. I can't wait to see what God has planned for you!

I love you guys, each of you and all of you. Our differences make us unique, and our love draws us together.

To God be the glory, now and forever. Amen.

☆-----☆

Introduction

My prayer for this book is that people would see my heart, the real me. I am nothing special, and I am nothing without God; but He promises that His power is made perfect and complete in us when we are the weakest and most incapable! So I am trusting Him to work and draw people closer to Himself, because nothing I say, do, or write can do that.

I hope you see my heart in this. I'm really just a girl who loves Jesus and is learning to trust more and more in Him. I've tried to be real throughout the pages of this book, and I hope you can be, too. Because when we start living the lives of love that God has planned for us, that is when amazing things start happening.

Stay you. But don't be afraid to change.

Love always,

Danae Jacobson

things
I've
learned
lately

I've learned that...

Summer is my favorite season,

Friends don't always have to get along,

Even important people take breaks,

And all little boys miss their mommies at bedtime.

I've learned that...

Life is short and death unthwartable,

Love is more than three words,

Chocolate chip cookies taste better as dough,

And you should never wait to tell someone

why you love them.

I've learned that...

I'm not home yet—I'm just passing through,

Time is never as important as people,

Smiles can make your day,

And happy times can come

hand in hand with sad ones.

I've learned that...

When you meet people,

You usually decide whether or not

You like them soon afterward,

People are precious,

The greatest of these really is love,

And I need to marry a sensitive person.

I've learned that...

Getting up twenty minutes earlier

gives you a better outlook on the day,

The color red can mean death and blood

or love and hearts,

Forgiving someone is proof of your love,

And respect isn't good enough for God.

I've learned that...

Some people are afraid to cry,

Relationships take work,

You really have to accept people as they are and

not try to change them

into what you think they should be,

And midnight laughter cleanses you.

I've learned that...

The stars shine brighter

when there is no moon,

Everyone has something

that makes their heart glad,

America is a country that

needs the prayers of her people,

And my mom understands.

I've learned that...

Dogs really are man's best friend—not so much

that they are ours, but we are theirs,

Heaven's got to be something special,

Coincidences are really "God things,"

And love always trusts, always hopes.

I've learned that...

The right thing is not always clear—both sides

may believe they're right,

but there are not two right ways,

There is a time for everything,

Being challenged to grow is a good thing,

And loving people is a gift.

I've learned that...

Looking people in the eyes

is a way of showing respect,

My grandma is my friend,

Pears bruise easily,

And the world can be a cold, hard place.

I've learned that...

We don't have to know everything,

The guy at church has known pain,

more than some know in a lifetime,

Country music isn't so bad after all,

And Christmas is love.

I've learned that...

Being around someone

wholly devoted to God is refreshing,

My horses trust me,

When our motivation is anything other than love,

then Christianity becomes merely a religion,

And my family is precious, more so than anything.

I've learned that...

When people are nervous,

they become someone other than themselves,

Work is necessary,

Sometimes life stinks,

And we all struggle—no one is

as confident as he seems.

I've learned that...

College might not be what I imagine,

Sometimes you have to let people go,

Having fun with someone

opens the door for friendship,

And everyone you meet has a life.

I've learned that...

Some people act older than they are,

Baby chicks grow up quickly,

We are immortal until God is ready for us to die,

And God has a plan.

I've learned that...

We usually take for granted the feelings

of people we don't understand,

Little girls need to feel pretty,

Books are like friends

who share a little of themselves with you,

And change is inevitable.

I've learned that...

It's always better to give people the benefit of

the doubt, although most of us don't,

Dogs' eyes show their trust and love,

B-ball is important to me,

And I never want to get too big

for a hug from my dad.

I've learned that...

There's so much more inside people than we see,

Everyone looks for love,

I love God,

And a good teacher is really a friend.

I've learned that...

Most people have the

same feelings and needs as me—

they just express them differently,

Everyone has faults,

And the best things in life are people.

I've learned that...

Memories are a treasure you should never let go,

Little boys need baths,

And what a person sees in you is sometimes very

different than what you think he's seeing.

Chocolate Chip Cookies
Taste Better As Dough

There's something about chocolate chip cookies that is special. Almost anyone can make them, whether or not you know much about baking. And if you don't burn the cookies or use two cups of baking soda instead of flour, they usually turn out pretty good.

Even better than the cookies, though, is the cookie dough. Sometimes my friends and I will get together to watch movies or listen to music while we make cookie dough instead of cookies. Forget the baking sheet—we dig right in with our spoons. And despite repeated warnings, none of us has ever gotten salmonella from the uncooked eggs.

Maybe it's because I usually eat dough with a bunch of friends while talking, laughing, and singing. Maybe it's because we grew up being told by Mom, "Don't eat the dough!" But whatever the reason, my friends and I agree that chocolate chip cookies definitely taste better as dough.

And you know what? I've learned that that's true about a lot of things in life. It's so easy to look ahead and imagine how wonderful life will be "when I get to college" or "when I turn twenty-one" or "when I get married." But today is all we are guaranteed. What if today *is* the best part? If we're always waiting for and dreaming about the finished product, we can miss out on what is really the best! So my advice and philosophy is to live in the now. Take a big bite of the cookie dough, and share it with someone you love.

The best and most beautiful things

cannot be seen or even touched.

They must be felt with the heart.

Helen Keller

> Meanwhile we groan, longing to be clothed
> with our heavenly dwelling.
>
> 2 CORINTHIANS 5:2

I'm Just Passing Through

When I walk down the halls of my high school, every once in a while it hits me how unsatisfied everyone seems. Even though many of the people are laughing and talking, I can tell they aren't content. They are longing for something more, something they don't have and can't even name.

At home, sometimes I look at my family and see the same desire and longing on their faces. When I walk down the sidewalk in our little town and smile at people as they pass, their smiles are short, not reaching their eyes. So many people I meet seem to be giving their all to *something*—a business, their religion, a relationship—but it's not enough to satisfy them.

Our world is full of unfulfilled people. Most don't know what they are so desperately longing for, while some of us don't realize that we are longing after anything at all. But more and more I'm convinced that this longing is part of being human—that when we are born, it is planted somewhere deep within us all.

I believe what we're talking about is really a longing for heaven. Because we belong to God, because we are His children, here on earth we will always feel a little out of place, a little unfulfilled, a little like strangers in a faraway land.

Paul writes in Philippians 3:20 that "our citizenship is in heaven." We were made for heaven; earth is only a temporary place. This dissatisfaction, this feeling that something is missing, is really our cry for home.

In heaven, no drunk drivers kill your best friend, no little children get sick or go hungry, no one is depressed or commits suicide, nobody cries for their love that was lost or never was, no secret fears come to terrorize you, no guilt remains, no one feels forgotten or unaccepted, no pain is present, and no tears fall except tears of joy.

Yes, heaven is perfect. But heaven will not satisfy us because it is so perfect or so unlike earth, but rather it will satisfy because of the Person who lives there. He's the one we're homesick for. David wrote, "I will see your face; when I awake, I will be satisfied" (Psalm 17:15).

When I see His face, *I'll know I'm home.*

In the meantime, I remind myself that I feel these longings for good reason. I was made for more than this world can ever offer, and I'm just passing through.

> I am fulfilled and yet I hunger.
> What means this deeper hunger in my heart?
>
> Alfred Noyes

Since no man knows the future,
who can tell him what is to come?

ECCLESIASTES 8:7

You Don't Have to Know Your Future to Have One

There is a question that every high school senior is asked at least a thousand times. If you're a senior or have ever been one, then you know which question I mean: "What are you going to do after you graduate?" or "Have you decided where you're going to college next year?" Both questions are essentially asking what you plan to do with the rest of your life.

Maybe you're one of the fortunate few that knows exactly how to answer. You know where you're going to college, what your major will be (always a follow-up question if you answer the first one correctly!), what profession you'll pursue, and even where you'll live and work *after* college. Some of my friends can tell you how many children they plan to have and whom they intend to marry.

But if you're like me and many others, you really don't have a clue about what comes next. When I first started being asked "the question," my answers varied. My plans changed weekly or even daily, depending on whom I was talking to or what ideas were going through my head at that moment. I always tried to find something to say—anything—even if it wasn't quite true. After all, aren't seniors supposed to know what they plan to do with their lives?

Then one night I was talking to my uncle about college. I told him I was thinking about taking a year off before I go. He thought that was a great idea, much to my surprise. He pointed out that so many people go to college right away because, well, that's just what everyone does. He also pointed out that college will always be there and that there are so many other things (like traveling or interning) that I might not be able to do if I wait until after college.

I still don't know exactly what my plans are, except that I hope to postpone college for a year. But since talking with my uncle, I think I have finally figured out how to answer the big question with passion and honesty. Next time a great-aunt from Washington or a complete stranger in the grocery checkout line asks me what I'm planning to do with my future, I'll thank her for caring and then tell her the truth: "I have absolutely no idea!"

If you happen to be a senior who's confused about your

future, take it from a girl who has been there: *It's okay not to know your plans!* It really is. In fact, saying "I don't know," instead of pretending you do know, frees you up to consider all kinds of different possibilities.

In the meantime, pray about your future every day. Take your parents' advice to heart (they usually have your best interests in mind). Talk to plenty of people about your options. And remember, God holds the answers to your future in His hands, and He'll get them from there to your head when He's ready.

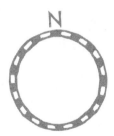

Our mouths were filled with laughter,
our tongues with songs of joy.
PSALM 126:2

Midnight Laughter Cleanses the Soul

We were bundled in our sleeping bags, gazing at the stars from the top of the houseboat. It was after midnight, and the rest of the boat was deathly quiet. We talked softly about the stars, love, and our dreams. One of us (I can't remember who) said something, and we all started giggling. We quickly shushed each other, but after a moment of reprimanded silence, someone giggled and set us off again. We soon moved from muffled giggles to outright, loud, from-the-stomach laughter. Our laughter was the only sound in the night, except for the gentle lapping of the water against the shore. We'd try to stop laughing and quiet ourselves, and we *would* settle down a little. But then one of us would start to say something, and we'd all start laughing again.

It was a silly cycle that seemed to have no end. When our

stomachs hurt so badly that we couldn't laugh without pain, then we stopped. Falling asleep that night, I was contented and at peace.

Another night I was with a friend and we were staying at my grandparents' house. We were sleeping in the guest bed, which is directly beneath my grandparents' room. As I got into bed, a voice called out, "Ouch! Get off! You're hurting me!" My friend and I started screaming until we realized there was some sort of mechanism somewhere on my side of the bed, and it was activated when weight was placed on it. After five or ten minutes of digging through the covers, we finally found the culprit, but that did nothing to calm us down. If anything, that little practical joke set the stage: We couldn't stop laughing.

Soon we were singing the Beach Boys' "California Girls" and "Surfer Girl" at the top of our lungs. We started making up songs in Spanish, all the while laughing hysterically. We were crazy, seriously wacky. If someone had videotaped or recorded us, our friends would probably disown us. An hour before we had both been tired and ready to sleep, but this was so much more fun! It was the most immature I'd acted in a long time, but given the same situation, I'd probably do it again. There's just something about it that was refreshing. I think both of us needed to just let go, forget, and laugh.

Times like these are so necessary. Afterward you feel cleansed, lighthearted. It's as though the zaniness and the laughter wash away all the dirty, difficult things in life. Your problems may or may not be there in the morning. But for a time, at least, you forget. And in those few moments, you know (or you're reminded) that the simple things in life, like midnight laughter, are the everyday miracles that matter most.

Live now, believe me,

wait not till tomorrow:

gather the roses of life today.

Pierre de Rosnand

> Finally, all of you, live in harmony with one another; be
> sympathetic, love as brothers, be compassionate and humble.
>
> 1 PETER 3:8

It's Best to Believe the Best

Recently I was with some friends and a couple of my cousins at a high school volleyball game. After it was over, we went out for milkshakes. My cousin told us he was exhausted and wanted to head home. I tried to convince him to come along, but it was obvious he wasn't going to join us. So the rest of us left for the restaurant.

A few minutes later, we were seated at a booth that looked out on the main street of our little town. We were all a little surprised when we saw my cousin's little silver pickup drive by, heading away from his house. While we finished our shakes, we talked about where he was really headed. Maybe back to the high school? Or to another friend's house? We concluded that he had obviously lied to us when he told us he was going home, probably in order to ditch us.

A few days later when I saw my cousin in town I asked him,

"Why did you lie to us the other day after the volleyball game?"

His expression was blank. "What are you talking about?"

"The other day when we were going to get milkshakes you said you were going home."

"Yeah, I did go home."

"Then how come we all saw you driving in the opposite direction of your house?" I knew my tone sounded accusatory, but I couldn't help it.

He just shook his head, and his eyes widened with surprise. "I was just going to get gas," he said.

Suddenly I felt like an immature child. I had basically told my cousin that I didn't really trust him, that I thought him a liar. Fortunately he forgave me quickly, but the incident reminded me that it's important to believe the best about people, to give them the benefit of the doubt until you know the full story.

It also got me wondering: *Why do I, and so many others I know, fail to give people we love the benefit of the doubt?*

Maybe because it hurts so much to believe in someone with all your heart and then have them let you down. It seems easier and safer to protect ourselves by assuming the worst right away, rather than believing the best about someone and then getting burned. At least this way, we avoid the pain of feeling like we've been played for a fool.

The problem with that approach, however, is that more

often than not, we *end up the fool,* as I did with my cousin. And in the process we hurt the feelings of the person we doubted. My dad often says we should "believe the best and accept less." Maybe that's the key. We can believe the best about the people we love, but also remember that we are all human and we all fail one another at times. Loving someone means always believing the best, but accepting less than the best and maybe even the worst.

So whether I end up with the best or the worst, either way I've decided that it's better to be wrong about believing the best than to be right about believing the worst.

A Good Book Is
Really a Friend

Ever since I've been able to sound out words, I've loved reading. Growing up, I read almost constantly—books like The Boxcar Children series, the Nancy Drew series, *Little House on the Prairie,* and the American Girls series. As I got older, my tastes changed, but never my love of reading.

Reading takes me to other places. Just a couple of days ago I found myself in a quiet valley in Montana, getting to know the local characters. And a few weeks ago I was in ancient Rome, caught up in the lives of gladiators, senators, and slaves. I become an observer in the lives of those the book is about. I picture the scenes clearly, almost as if the setting were a real place, or as if I'm watching a play. Maybe that's why seeing a movie adaptation after reading the book can be so disappointing. Everything is always very different from how you imagined it.

Often when I've finished a book, I feel like the stories

actually took place and the characters were real people. When I turn the last page, I sometimes feel sad because I don't want the story to be over. I want to continue being a part of the characters' lives.

Maybe my passion for books sounds a little excessive. But I've come to realize that there's a good reason for it. Not only are there adventures to be had and lessons to be learned, but there are friends to be made. I shall, for example, always share a certain bond with Anne Shirley *(Anne of Green Gables)* because of our mutual love for writing and the search for beautiful, romantic things. I will always wish I could've lived in the same era as Laura Ingalls Wilder *(Little House on the Prairie),* and I've often wondered what she would think if she were transported to the future and into my life. And I hope that I will be like Elizabeth Bennet *(Pride and Prejudice),* who was finally able to see past the surface and into the heart of the man she would grow to love.

C. S. Lewis said, "If you do not read good books, you have no advantage over the one who does not read at all." There are countless books out there, but many of them are not "good books" and therefore are not worth reading. But there are also many excellent books and writers that can touch your soul.

The next time you're bored, instead of watching TV, grab a good book that interests you and see what happens. Who knows what faraway lands you may travel to or what people you will meet. Maybe you'll find yourself immersed in another world, laughing and crying with the new friends you've made through the pages of a book.

We read to know

that we are not alone.

C. S. Lewis

You will fill me with joy in your presence,
with eternal pleasures at your right hand.

PSALM 16:11

It's Good to Do Nothing with God

Tonight I was outside feeding my horses, and my rottweiler, Dillon, was with me. Everywhere I went he followed me, exploring every inch of the ground. He chased the chickens and just stared at our foal until she ran behind her mother. When I finished my chores, I walked over to the lawn and picked up a ball. The moment I touched it, Dillon's ears perked up. Anticipating my throw, he nabbed the ball and proudly danced across the lawn with the ball wedged in his mouth, staying just out of my reach. I chased him all over, but I couldn't catch him.

When I got tired and gave up, he trotted happily over and nudged me with his nose. I sat on the grass and watched the moon, not fully visible as the sun hadn't yet set, and Dillon plopped down beside me. His head rested on my legs, and he gazed up contentedly at me, his prize still in his mouth. I sat stroking his thick, black fur and scratching his velvety ears. I began to sing quietly, and every few minutes he would look up at me. I have never seen a look like that before. His brown eyes were so kind, so happy and trusting. It was almost as if he was saying "Thank you for petting me" and "I love you."

The ball slipped out of Dillon's mouth as he relaxed more and more. When he looked at me, I could see his contentment. I knew, just from that look, how much he loves me and loves being with me. He said more with his eyes than some people say in a whole day using words.

It hit me then that you can learn a lot about God from a dog. So many times we get caught up in "doing" for God instead of simply being with Him. Yes, I know God loves it when He sees us out there actively living for and serving Him. But I also know that our Father loves it even more when we lay our heads in His lap, look up at Him with adoring eyes, and do nothing but enjoy being with Him.

†

Trying to Change a Friend Isn't Fair

A few months ago, someone said something that has stuck with me ever since. I was talking with my cousin, complaining about her refusal to come to my sixteenth birthday party. I begged her for a long time to come, but she had made it very clear that parties just aren't her thing. She prefers being in small groups or with just one person. I know this about her. Regardless, I selfishly continued to bug her about the party. And then one day she said, "Danae, I'm sorry that I'm not who you want me to be, but I can't change that and neither can you."

I couldn't find any words to say. I finally saw what I had been doing, and I felt horrible. I've always loved my cousin dearly, but I hadn't really been acting like it. I was trying to force her to do something that she wasn't comfortable with, which not only hurt her but also damaged our friendship. She reminded me that our friendship is what is most important, not a birthday party that would last for only a few hours.

Maybe you've been in a similar situation. Maybe you have a friend who absolutely refuses to be seen in a bathing suit. Or maybe there's a friend who always tells jokes you think are really dumb.

It's tempting to try to change our friends, and our motives may seem noble and unselfish. We want the best for our friends, and we truly think that it would be good for them to learn to dance, try to water-ski, or whatever. But when we put our friends on a self-improvement program we've designed, it's likely to backfire. (Think about how you feel when someone tries to get you to do something that seems fundamentally at odds with who you are.)

In the end, when you're tempted to try to change your friends, that's probably a sign that you should do the exact opposite. Accept them exactly as they are—that's always the best thing for everyone.

> If a man loudly blesses his neighbor
> early in the morning,
> it will be taken as a curse.
>
> PROVERBS 27:14

It's a Morning Person's World

As far back as King Solomon's day, it was undeniable: God made some to be morning people and some to be night people. (Read Proverbs 27:14—Solomon was obviously a night person.)

We've all met morning people, folks who are always happy, no matter what time they went to bed or what time they got up. They tend to wear the biggest, cheeriest smiles—especially, it seems, when nonmorning people like me are still trying to wake up.

Then there are the night people. Night people regularly stay up (often alone) way past midnight, doing whatever it is night people do. They then sleep through half the daylight hours, getting up around noon and repeating the cycle.

Rarely are these nocturnal people awake during what most people would consider morning.

I confess that I have been known to yell at people I don't even know simply because they were being, in my mind, excessively cheerful before lunch. However, I do not exhibit all the usual traits of a night person. The reason? When you're a teenager who happens to be a night person, it's pretty much impossible to fulfill your destiny—the world is set up in such a way as to cruelly interfere with your natural inclinations.

For example, school begins at 8 A.M., not at noon. And after a certain hour on weeknights, there's really nothing to do and no one else awake to keep you company, even if you weren't so exhausted from being awakened at the outrageously early hour of six-thirty.

Let's face it: It's a morning person's world. That being said, for many years I have given no guarantees regarding my disposition in the morning, particularly if you are the one with the unenviable task of waking me up. (Nonmorning people rarely respond to alarm clocks.)

For a long time, the way I coped was to be silent on the subject. My basic philosophy was taken from Thumper's mother in the movie *Bambi:* "If you can't say somethin' nice, don't say nothin' at all." I figured that keeping my mouth shut would give me a chance to wake up slowly. Then I wouldn't say things I would regret once I was fully human, and I could gradually become more sociable as the day wore on. By lunchtime I might be able to say something that, although not exactly uplifting and encouraging, was at least not cruel or sarcastic.

Unfortunately, this technique didn't always work. It's hard to stay quiet when someone very irritating—a brother or mother or sister or, well, anyone at all—starts talking to you or asking you completely unnecessary questions in what seems to you a loud volume or grating tone. Naturally, there were times when, no matter how hard I tried, my vow of silence failed (often in a very bad way).

My family was fairly patient, considering my wild outbursts when they slipped up and accidentally spoke to me. One day my dad kindly suggested that I get up earlier. That way I would have more time to wake up and less need to rush. Maybe a slower pace in the morning would be the cure.

At first I thought the idea was ludicrous. Who wants to get up *earlier?* No one—except, of course, morning people. But for lack of any alternative, and not wanting to be thrown out of my family, I decided to try it. And surprisingly, it worked! Something about those extra twenty minutes before I see people lets me awaken fully and become myself—my better self, that is.

I know it sounds crazy, but if, like me, you're not a morning person, give it a try. Maybe you need only five minutes. Or maybe forty-five. Whatever it takes, try to get up a bit earlier. When I do, the things in life that are important to me shine through. And often when I don't, my nonmorning-person haziness tends to distort reality—for myself and everyone who has the misfortune of encountering me.

And for all you morning people out there who are laughing at us nonmorning people, go ahead and keep being cheery. We understand that's how God made you. But maybe you could restrain yourselves the *tiniest* bit—for all our sakes.

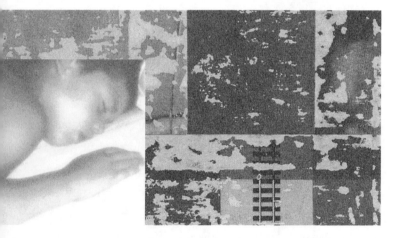

> Jesus said to them, "My Father is always at his work
> to this very day, and I, too, am working."
>
> JOHN 5:17

Coincidences Are Really "God Things"

Just last night I was at a party with a bunch of people. Everyone was having a wonderful time just being together and having fun. But for some reason I was having a hard night, and I just couldn't seem to join in the fun.

I went outside to be by myself, to think and try to figure out what exactly was bothering me. While I was out there I started crying, and I asked God for somebody to talk to. I didn't even know how to express what was bothering me, but I knew I needed to talk to *someone* about it.

I walked back inside, and immediately one of my friends came up and gave me this huge hug. I sat beside her for a long time, trying to figure out how to explain to her what I was feeling. Eventually I just started talking, and it *just so happened* that she had been bothered by exactly the same thing. Words weren't necessary. We both were feeling the same way, and when one of us would say something, the other would say, "It's the same for me" or "That's exactly how I feel."

I guess it would be easy to brush this off as a mere coincidence. But really, of all my friends that were there that I could have talked to, she was the one I ended up with. And of all my friends, with all their different problems, she was the one who understood and was experiencing the very same feelings as me. Amazing!

I've learned to look at occurrences like these and see God in them. Sure, it's easy to become hardened and cynical, to doubt that something good happened because Someone actually planned it. But when we start recognizing that those little things in our lives are more than just coincidences, that's when life gets fun.

When "coincidences" happen in my life, I would rather believe they come from Someone who has had a plan for my life since the beginning of time than believe that they happened by random chance. It is not just that I would rather believe that God takes an interest in me because it's more comforting; some things simply cannot be explained any other way.

Our lives are full of these moments, big and small, these *God things,* whether or not we see them or want to admit it. I believe God is just waiting for you to realize that it's Him who set up the "chance" encounter that led to finding your true love and that it's Him who made the almost-car-accident not happen. I think God really loves it when people stop calling these moments coincidences and start calling them "God things." God delights in giving good gifts to His children—He just wants us to know who they're from.

A Friend Doesn't Have
to Be Near to Be Close

Last year a bunch of my friends graduated. All through high school, we had been very close; but when they graduated, things began changing. The summer after their graduation everything was basically the same as it had always been. We were all very busy working and going places with our families, but we were together a lot of the time when we were home. The summer went by more quickly than any I had known, and then it was time for me to go back to school.

While I was at school each day, my alumni friends were either working or taking college classes. I quickly became involved again with the happenings at my high school, and my free time was spent doing homework, going to basketball practice, watching football games, and hanging out with friends from class. My friends who had graduated would try to call me, but I was usually gone or busy with one of these things.

As the weeks passed, I didn't get as many messages on the machine or from my mom that my old friends had called. I would see them somewhere, and we would promise to do something soon, but then it would be weeks until I saw them again.

This change was hard, and it still makes me a little sad when I think about it. I miss how it used to be with all of us. I realize that I am the one who has been busy, the one who has pulled away. But that doesn't mean I miss them any less.

Maybe you have experienced this, too. A friendship changes over time as the two of you are pulled in different directions. In order to keep living and becoming who you are, you have to let go. Sometimes it feels a little like you are giving up or even betraying the friendship. But I'm learning it doesn't have to be that way at all.

The other day I ran into one of those friends at the video store. Our conversation was awkward and stilted for a moment. She was very tan and had a new boyfriend, but other than that, things seemed the same on the outside. Then we got to really talking, and I realized that nothing had changed in our hearts. From what my mom tells me, it will probably feel the same way when I'm thirty. I'll run into a friend I let go of years ago, and after a single conversation, I'll feel as close to her as ever.

That's reassuring to know, isn't it? Time passes; people move on; friendships change. But although sometimes we have to let go of a person's presence or nearness, that doesn't mean we ever have to let go of the love or the friendship.

Be slow in choosing a friend,

slower in changing.

Benjamin Franklin

"God Bless America" Is More than a Song

Yesterday after school my sister and her friend burst into the house singing "The Star Spangled Banner" at the top of their lungs. A year ago, it would have struck me as a little strange to hear two junior-high-age girls singing our national anthem rather than the latest number one hit on the radio. But now it's yet another reminder of the patriotism that is rampant throughout our land since the tragic events of September 11. Everywhere I look I see the signs: flags on cars; red, white, and blue pins on clothing; and the phrase "God bless America" everywhere.

Before the war on terror that we are now waging, patriotic would not have been a word to describe many

Americans. Many fans listened almost grudgingly as the national anthem was sung at baseball games, or they'd stare disinterestedly at the flag for lack of anything else to look at during the song. But ever since my mom woke me up early on the morning of September 11 to watch the news, things have changed in a big way.

Suddenly, it is no longer corny to be patriotic. Last Friday night I watched grown men cry as my friend sang the national anthem at the high school football game. Many of my friends have flag stickers on the backs of their cars. At professional basketball games, more emphasis is placed on "The Star Spangled Banner," "America, the Beautiful," and the true heroes (firefighters and police officers) than on announcing the players.

I love watching our country's people come together and truly be united. Our flag is revered, our freedoms are treasured, and our leaders are honored. "God Bless America" has become more than just a meaningful song. These days, it is the cry of our nation and for many a heartfelt prayer.

All beautiful you are, my darling; there is no flaw in you.
You have stolen my heart, my sister, my bride;
you have stolen my heart with one glance of your eyes,
with one jewel of your necklace.

SONG OF SONGS 4:7, 9

Romance Is Underrated

He may have written his love poem thousands of years ago, but King Solomon clearly understood that women want to be romanced.

There's just something that stirs a girl's heart when a guy sings "I Do (Cherish You)" to you, brings you a huge bouquet of flowers with a note telling you what he loves about you, or puts a box of chocolates from a "secret admirer" on your car.

But why do romantic gestures like these matter so much to us?

If you stop and think about it, those cards or notes are just paper and words; the flowers are just a plant that grew in the ground; and the chocolates are tasty, but while we're saying, "Thank you!" on the outside, we're secretly thinking, *Are you serious? Do you want me to gain ten pounds?!*

So what is the longing for romance all about? Obviously, it's not the actual gift or the card that matters, but something else. It's the feeling and emotion behind the gifts and cards. It's the fact that the guy took the time to find a way to say "I love you" or "I think you're special." It makes a girl feel as if she's being pursued, wooed, wanted, and appreciated.

I'm not sure most guys understand this, which is probably why most of them think romance is overrated. At the beginning of any relationship, of course, this usually isn't the case. My friend Kali had a boyfriend who was incredibly sweet, sensitive, and romantic. Almost every day she'd find a note on her car, at work, or at her locker. And every time they went out he always brought her flowers. But as the months passed, the notes and surprises gradually subsided. By the time they broke up, he wasn't even opening doors for her or calling when he said he would, much less bringing her flowers and leaving notes on her car.

Certainly there are wonderful guys out there to whom this doesn't apply, but in my experience and that of my friends, the gradual waning of romance has been the rule. Maybe most guys let romance slip because they don't realize how much it means to the girl. They don't understand that it takes only the tiniest bit of effort on the part of a guy to make a girl feel cherished and special. Most guys, once they're pretty sure they've "got the girl," forget that she still wants to be pursued.

I've seen this happen a lot with married people, too. I understand that marriage is completely different than just dating someone. I realize that marriage isn't an easy thing; in fact, it's probably one of the hardest things. However, I don't think that after marriage things should become less romantic. If anything it should become more so because you know the other person even better.

I want to marry a guy who will be romantic with me long after we've grown old and gray—a guy who will keep doing all the little things and keep doing them from his heart. I want somebody who thinks romance is highly *underrated.* I'm going to wait as long as I have to in order to find the guy who will sing me "I Do (Cherish You)," mean what he's singing, and sing it for the rest of our lives.

No one has ever seen God; but if we love one another,
God lives in us and his love is made complete in us.

1 JOHN 4:12

Love Slows Down to Really See

I watch my littlest brother play quietly with my sister. Together they build a house made of blankets and pillows for their cats. Their quiet giggles drift over to where I stand, unnoticed. I walk away and leave them to their play.

★--★

My mom and dad share a tender kiss and embrace when they think we're all occupied elsewhere. The look in their eyes tells me more of their love than words ever could, and I tiptoe away quietly.

★--★

I see my other brother sitting on the couch, lost in his book. He laughs out loud at something he reads, surprising himself. He looks up and gives me a self-conscious little grin. "Listen to this, Danae," he says, as he reads the words that made him laugh. We share a laugh together over it, and then we talk for a few minutes about nothing important. I go upstairs to my room and leave him to enjoy his book.

★--★

In my room, I replay these scenes in my mind. I smile and brush away a tear. They are simple things, really—houses for cats, kisses, and books—just small, quiet, ordinary moments with my family. On most days, I might have rushed impatiently past and missed them altogether. But lately, as my mind is filled with thoughts of graduation, college, and moving away, I've been learning that if I let love slow me down long enough, I'll really see my family—and I will realize how precious they are to me.

Stillness is what creates love.

Movement is what creates life.

To be still and still moving, this is everything.

Unknown

> "See how the lilies of the field grow. They do not labor
> or spin. Yet I tell you that not even Solomon
> in all his splendor was dressed like one of these."
>
> MATTHEW 6:28—29

Ordinary Life Is a Beautiful Thing

Like most kids, when I was very young I always put famous athletes and movie stars in a whole different category than ordinary people. I was in awe of athletes like Michael Jordan and Marion Jones, and I don't think I even believed Julia Roberts was human.

As I grew older, I became a little more realistic about famous people. I knew that they began life like any "normal" person. Yet I was keenly aware that they had been propelled into a huge spotlight, and in my eyes, this made them anything but ordinary. It was hard to imagine that their lives could ever be less than wonderful. I mean, they have nice clothes and nice cars—not to mention that they are beautiful people.

Then one day while I was shopping with a friend and trying on crazy outfits, confident that no one in the store knew us or would ever see us again, it hit me. *Famous people can't do stuff like this.* And the more I thought about it, the more I realized that there are many things—simple, everyday things that bring me joy—that busy, famous people can't do, or at least can't do easily.

For example, just being with my friends, sitting on my bed for hours and doing nothing but talking and laughing. Going to high school football games and cheering as loud as anyone. Spending a day with my mom, shopping at all the cute little tourist attractions and antiques stores. Going to a movie on Saturday night and getting some ice cream at Baskin-Robbins afterward. Or even going to a store and trying on wild outfits with a friend.

These things are hard to do when people recognize you everywhere you go (unless you wear a disguise). Fans expect you to be happy constantly and to always look the way you do in the magazines and on TV. Even your friends probably imagine you're too busy to laugh over nothing for hours. And something like a simple Saturday-night movie can easily turn into a grueling, three-hour autograph session.

I cannot imagine living like that, despite the obvious benefits. Now every time I hear a celebrity talk about her life, instead of focusing on the glamorous bits, I keep in mind that she still has to shave her legs, wake up when the alarm goes off, and work hard at whatever it is she does in order to stay on top. I notice more often her comments about all the traveling she must do, the difficulty of keeping her long-distance relationship together, her constant worry about what she eats and how her skin looks, or her feelings of anger and hurt about the lies being published about her.

I'm not saying that fame is all bad or even that it's something to avoid. I believe that if God called a person to be famous, He would give him or her the strength necessary to cope with the hard parts and to appreciate that life.

But when you think about it, being ordinary really isn't all that bad. In fact, you might even say it has a glamour all its own.

The art of being happy lies in the power of extracting happiness from common things.

Henry Ward Beecher

Good Friends Aren't Afraid to Fight

When I was eleven, I made my first real "best friends." Sally and Erin lived nearby, and they loved horses and reading as much as I did. During one summer, the three of us became inseparable. We made all kinds of promises, secret clubs, and pacts. Our time was spent hanging out at the barn, racing our horses, swimming in the pond and in their pool, riding our bikes, and staying the night at each other's houses. In my mind, this was exactly as it should be with best friends.

There was just one problem: I was so determined that nothing would ever come between us in the way of disagreements that I went to extremes to keep the peace. Whenever a potential mis-understanding or difference of opinion popped up, I would quickly take the blame and say I was wrong. Sometimes these little arguments were about silly things, like what one of us had said or what we would do that day. But other times they would involve more important things, like religion or what we believed was right and wrong.

Looking back now, I see that each time I didn't (or

wouldn't) speak up, each time I withheld my true thoughts and feelings, I created an invisible distance between me and my friends. Ironically, because I feared that being honest would lead to losing my friends, I sacrificed the kind of honesty that holds real friendships together.

Eventually, Sally and Erin moved away. And although nothing big ever happened to divide us, over time we've drifted apart.

Being honest with friends, even when it's hard, is a lesson I seem to relearn over and over. I keep making the mistake of thinking that friends must always get along and should never have conflicts.

Recently, one of my close friends—we'll call him Mark—did some things that really made me mad. I felt like he lied to me about a relationship he was in. And being lied to by a friend, no matter what it's about, is one of the worst feelings there is.

Frustrated and hurt, I vented to a couple of other friends. Both told me to talk to him, but I didn't want to risk a conflict. Mark had no idea that something was wrong, and to me it seemed better to leave it that way. I would rather try to forget the incident than make it into a huge deal.

Then one afternoon, Sally and Erin popped into my mind, and I realized that I was doing it again. By not being honest with Mark, I was being unfair to him. After all, no one can apologize or try to change his behavior if he has no idea there's something wrong.

After thinking it through, I decided to call Mark that night and discuss what happened. It wasn't easy, but it was the best thing I could have done. We talked about the issue, clarified some details, and when we hung up there was a genuine connection and closeness between us that hadn't been there in a while.

It's all too easy when we're offended or hurt by a friend to pull away from that person or tell others or pretend that nothing has happened. But real friendship can happen only when we are fully honest and transparent with one another, even when it might cause conflict.

It's good to know that friends don't always have to get along. And once in a while, it's probably good if they don't.

> True friendship multiplies the good in life and divides its evils.
>
> Baltasar Gracian

Country Music
Isn't So Bad after All

I was born in a big city, but I've spent most of my life in a town whose population count is 911. We live two hours from a major city and are considered by most to be either country folk or hicks. (The latter, however, is not something we like being called.)

Almost every adult in the area listens to one of three country music radio stations, and all of the local kids complain about the lack of other "good" stations. For a long time that was me—constantly flipping the radio knobs to find songs that were acceptable and definitely *not* country-western. I knew all the places in my town where the big-city stations came in somewhat clearly.

Unfortunately, there were times when listening to country music was unavoidable. For example, when I was driving with someone I didn't know very well, or when my dad was in the mood for country music and couldn't be swayed. During these times I fumed silently and tried my best not to listen. But gradually, somehow, it happened. To my amazement, I heard a few country-western songs I actually liked.

How could this be? What was happening to me? I thought it must be time to move back to Portland before I started wearing a cowboy hat and Wranglers and saying "y'all."

Most of the songs I enjoyed were the soft, slow love songs, and I decided they weren't *really* country. But as I began to listen to country stations now and then, trying to find the sweet songs I liked, to my surprise I liked a lot of the other stuff I heard, too.

I dreaded the day when I would have to tell my dad about my change of heart. Of course, when I finally did, he teased me mercilessly for weeks. After all, I had been among the worst critics of his own taste for country music.

These days the tables have turned. Whenever I ask him if he likes someone's new song, he says something like, "Sorry, I haven't heard it yet." Now I am the one trying to get *him* to listen to more country. When Trisha Yearwood came to a town near ours, it was me, not my dad, who showed up at the concert.

So I guess you can call me a "country girl" if you want to, because I'm now completely hooked on country music. Songs like Tim McGraw's "Don't Take the Girl," Lee Ann Womack's "I Hope You Dance," and Steve Wariner's "Holes in the Floor of Heaven" will always be among my favorites.

I say all this not to convert you, but simply to point out that things we think we hate can become things we love. But it won't happen if you worry too much about what other people think. I listen to country music because I truly enjoy it, not because someone else thinks it's cool.

It also won't happen if you don't try it. How often do we say we hate things that we've never really tried? Maybe it's a sport, a hobby, or a kind of food. Maybe if you tried it, you'd discover you have a talent for skateboarding. Or maybe if you went once to a performance, you would fall completely in love with opera. Hey, you might as well try it. Maybe you'll even find that you like country music after all.

> Instruct a wise man and he will be wiser still; teach a
> righteous man and he will add to his learning.
>
> PROVERBS 9:9

You Can Learn a Lot from Bad Teachers

As a little girl, I remember seeing my first-grade teacher, Mrs. Karls, at the bank. I was shocked. There she was, standing in line, wearing shorts, a tank top, and sunglasses. I had never thought of Mrs. Karls as a real person with a life outside of school, someone who had to do things like run errands and use money. My six-year-old brain had permanently relegated her to the classroom.

Naturally, by the time I got to high school, I realized that teachers are normal people with lives like the rest of us. They have bad-hair days, lose their car keys, and visit the dentist. They feel insecure, want to lose weight, and go through divorces. Living in a small town, I see my teachers at church on Sunday, at the store, and even at the movies on Friday night.

But there's a downside to recognizing that teachers are

human. Eventually we discover that teachers also have faults like the rest of us. Sometimes high school teachers are crabby, forget to grade papers, or seem to have developed a strong dislike of anyone between the ages of twelve and twenty. Perhaps most surprising is when we realize that *some of them aren't very good at what they do and don't like it besides.*

We've all had the infamous boring teachers who do little other than assign reading and busywork. Their classes are endured but never anticipated. Their lectures don't stimulate discussions or even raised hands. Somewhere along the way they seem to have fallen into "auto-teach" mode.

I remember one teacher in particular. We'll call him Mr. Parker. I don't think he made eye contact with me once or called me by the right name the whole semester I was in his class. Most of Mr. Parker's energies seemed to go into drinking a thermos of coffee every period. (He obviously had as much trouble staying awake in his class as we did.) I figured, *Why make any effort to learn if the teacher obviously isn't trying to teach?* But at some point I realized that I wasn't in school to learn for *his* sake.

As I prepare for college, I'm coming to understand that learning doesn't have so much to do with how good a teacher is, but whether or not you choose to learn. Even if you have a bad teacher, you can still choose to be a good learner. And if you don't at least try, you'll never know what you're missing. What if you discover years down the road that you love history, but because of a bad teacher, you lost interest and missed out on years of learning?

Obviously it's easier to learn from a great teacher. But keep in mind that the chance to grow in knowledge is always there. And who knows? Maybe your interest in a subject will be just the spark a teacher needs to reignite his or her own enthusiasm. Maybe the Mr. Parker in your school (being human and probably aware of his shortcomings) could use an encouraging word. It just might make his day. Or it just might make *yours.*

Perfection is not attainable,

but if we chase perfection,

we can catch excellence.

Vince Lombardi

> The race is not to the swift or the battle to the strong, nor does food come to the wise or wealth to the brilliant or favor to the learned; but time and chance happen to them all.
>
> ECCLESIASTES 9:11

Life Is Unfair, but God Is Good

When someone I love is hurting, I always find myself asking, *Why?*

For example, it doesn't make sense that my beautiful, blond baby cousin, Avonléa, was born blind and with severe disabilities. As I write this, she is a little over six months old, yet she may never be able to do anything more that what she can right now, mentally or physically. When I think about the life she will probably lead, I can't help but ask God, *Why?*

I know God tells us that there is a time and a season for everything. But why does there have to be a time for bad things? Why was there a time for the Holocaust? Why the Ku Klux Klan? Why a time for Columbine? Why did my friend try to kill himself? Why are there little girls without daddies, and why are there little girls with daddies who hurt them? Why do freak accidents kill innocent people? The list is endless. Why?

It seems so wrong when someone has more than his or her "fair share" of heartache and tragedy. My best friend has had just about the hardest year I could imagine. Seeing the pain she's gone through, the pain that has taken her family and tried to destroy it, makes me cry for her. She's only seventeen. Why should she have to go through all that?

As I struggle with these issues, I wonder if everybody reaches this point eventually—the point when you realize that life truly is unfair. This is not the kind of unfairness you screamed about when you were four and didn't get a red Popsicle like your sister. This is the kind of unfairness you scream about when you get a phone call at 1:47 in the morning telling you that your friend was killed in an car accident with a drunk driver.

Bad things can happen to anyone for seemingly no reason. You can ask why as many times as you want, and you'll never really get the answer you're looking for.

But lately I'm beginning to wonder if *Why?* is the right question, if *What now?* might be a better one. No matter what bad things happen to those I love, to me, or to anyone in the world, I know that God has not left us alone. God still cares. God is good. Only He can bring something good out of something awful in people's lives—if they're willing to cooperate with Him.

Recently I read *Night* by Elie Wiesel, the famous Holocaust survivor. The things he saw and lived through in a German concentration camp as a fifteen-year-old boy were horrific, and they destroyed the faith and lives of many men three times his age. The word *senseless* seems to describe what happened perfectly. Yet when I consider what Wiesel has done with that nightmare, what necessary, righteous outrage his books have inspired, I'm amazed at how much good came out of the evil he endured.

My dad always says this about bad times: "You have two options. One, you can complain about the bad things in your life that you can't change, making yourself and those around you miserable. Or two, you can take the bad things that happen and try to discover what good God can bring out of them."

He's right. We've all seen people who go through life taking option number one. They spend so much time complaining and asking *Why?* that they get bitter and miss the beauty of life altogether.

I want to make the second choice, which is the one my aunt and uncle have made. As I've spent time with them and the rest of their kids, I've discovered that they don't see Avonléa's disabilities as this horrible thing that has happened. They see my cousin as a precious gift and a wonderful blessing. And I have to agree. I've seen people in my family, in my school, and in the community come together around her in a way they never would have otherwise.

Sometimes when I hold Avonléa and she smiles up at me, for a second I forget she is blind, and I imagine she can see me smiling back at her.

Sometimes I wonder if we're not all a little bit like her. Right now, on this side of heaven, we're often blinded to the good in our lives by the bad things that happen. We suffer and we feel alone. But all the while God is holding us close, smiling at us, wanting us to experience His blessing and perfect plan for our lives, and hoping we are aware of His love.

Have courage for the great sorrows of life and
patience for the small ones:
and when you have laboriously accomplished
your daily task, go to sleep in peace. God is awake.

Victor Hugo

And we know that in all things God works
for the good of those who love Him,
who have been called according to His purpose.

Romans 8:28

But the angel said to them, "Do not be afraid. I bring you good news of great joy that will be for all the people. Today in the town of David a Savior has been born to you; he is Christ the Lord. This will be a sign to you: You will find a baby wrapped in cloths and lying in a manger."

LUKE 2:10-12

Christmas Really Is about Gifts

What images come to your mind when you hear the word *Christmas?*

I think of snowflakes, twinkling lights, red cheeks, hot chocolate with marshmallows, overcrowded malls, Salvation Army volunteers ringing their bells, piles of pictures and letters from people you only hear from at Christmas, holiday sweaters, nights so cold your breath hangs in the air, locked closets and "off-limits" rooms, carolers, nativity scenes, Christmas Eve church services, poinsettias, icicles, reindeer, eggnog, and all kinds of sweet things that you never get the rest of the year.

My list could go on for pages, as I'm sure yours could. But even though I love the lights, the trees, and the snow, and even though those things will always be a part of what Christmas means to me, my reasons for loving Christmas are changing with every passing year.

These days, one of my favorite things about the Christmas season is how differently people treat each other. Have you noticed? At Christmastime, even though we all still have problems, people seem to focus more on the positive and make an effort to be kind to others. I've heard my parents lament, "If only you kids were this good all year." Others say, "The world would be a better place if people acted all the time like they do at Christmas."

Another thing that has changed is how I feel about Christmas presents. Sure, like all teens, I still like the presents that I get (especially since over the years I've moved from dolls and Play-doh to CDs, wakeboards, and clothes). But now, no matter how many presents I get or how expensive they are, they pale in comparison with the free gifts—things like seeing my little brother's sleepy smile when he first gets up Christmas morning, knowing that somewhere a little girl has a present to open on Christmas because I plucked her name from the gift tree at Target, or sharing my sister's excitement and sleeping by the tree on Christmas Eve.

I'm gradually coming to understand that the best reason to love Christmas is that it represents a dream bigger than any one person. It's a dream that love and mercy and goodwill won't be limited to the holidays. It's a dream that people everywhere will treasure the free gifts in life the most. And it's a dream of the day we will all meet the One who *is* the very essence of Christmas, the true reason we celebrate, and the greatest gift ever given.

An honest answer is like a kiss on the lips.

PROVERBS 24:26

Sometimes Others See Us Better than We See Ourselves

A few years ago I went to a new school as a freshman. One of my teachers there was a family friend. My dad came to me one day and asked me how I thought I was doing at school, but I knew he didn't just mean schoolwork and grades. I said I was fine, and then he told me that he'd talked to our friend about me.

"She was worried about you, Danae, because she sees you changing and the changes aren't for the positive." As we talked more, it become apparent that there wasn't a huge problem; it was little things like being rebellious, having an attitude, and trying to be like other people. What my dad said next is something I'll never forget. "Danae," he said softly, "sometimes our best pictures of ourselves are through other people."

He didn't accuse me of anything; he just gave me something to think about. I did think about it, and when I did, I realized that my teacher was right. Nothing was hugely wrong. What bothered me most wasn't even that something *was* wrong but rather that I had thought everything was fine. Perspectives are funny things. Sometimes it takes seeing ourselves as someone else sees us to truly see who we are and how we're living.

These clearer pictures of ourselves are not always for the worse. I've seen the kindest, most wonderful people break down crying because they don't believe they are doing anyone any good at all, when in reality they have touched so many lives in incredible ways.

So I think we all need to see ourselves through someone else's eyes every once in a while, whether it's a painful and difficult experience or a joyful and encouraging one. The hard part is taking what you hear, whether good or bad, and accepting it or learning from it. And although it's tough, I would rather know the truth than think I'm doing fine and really be doing horribly. Likewise, I would want to be told if I was doing something good and worthwhile and hadn't fully realized it.

So ask someone you trust how *they* see you. Encourage that person to give you an honest answer. You just might be surprised.

> The real voyage of discovery
> consists not in seeking new landscapes,
> but having new eyes.

Marcel Proust

Jesus wept.
JOHN 11:35

People Should Cry More Often

At the risk of reinforcing the stereotype that girls are more emotional than boys, I have to tell you that, like most girls I know, I cry on a fairly regular basis. I'm not an excessively emotional person, but I cry at the sweet parts in movies, when I'm tired and stressed, when I feel hurt by someone, or when something good or special happens.

Not surprisingly, most of the guys I know rarely, if ever, cry—especially in public. But what many people don't realize is that girls are often just as resistant as guys to cry openly. Most people seem to think it's okay if they quietly cry into their pillow at night or let a tear slip down their cheek at a movie. But if they shed tears in broad daylight, most people apologize and feel terrible that they "cried all over" a friend. They get embarrassed, as if crying were a thing to be ashamed of.

I wish it weren't like that. When people feel like they have to apologize for crying, they are essentially apologizing for what they feel, which is sad because you cannot help what you feel. Crying is necessary and healing. Sometimes the only thing to do is bury your head in a pillow or a friend's arms and just let everything out. Only when we cry, emptying ourselves of all the junk, can the space be filled with other, better things.

Wouldn't it be great if we lived in a world where it was considered okay to cry, whether from joy or grief or even just tiredness? What if we could all rest in the knowledge that tears are okay and that we are loved and accepted—blotchy faces, red noses, smeared makeup, sniffles, and all?

As strange as it sounds, I plan to do my part to make the world a more tearful place (or at least to make those who cry in front of me feel more comfortable about it). But as far as having a world where everyone feels free and comfortable to cry whenever the urge hits, I guess we won't see that until heaven. There the only tears we'll cry will be tears of joy, and you can bet that nobody will apologize for those.

> How great is the love the Father has lavished on us, that we
> should be called children of God! And that is what we are!
>
> 1 JOHN 3:1

All Little Boys Miss Their Mommies at Bedtime

I have always enjoyed baby-sitting and do it frequently for my own siblings, who are usually pretty well behaved. I didn't realize how well behaved they really are until I baby-sat for the Stevensons. (Note: The names in this story have been changed to protect the backsides of two little boys.)

Michael was six and Aaron was nine. They seemed like nice little boys. Michael had his mom's blond curls, and Aaron had a charmer's smile. I could tell this job would be a breeze.

Then the parents walked out the door.

Almost immediately, as if someone had pushed a panic button, Michael and Aaron turned into little terrors. They became uncontrollably wild. All through dinner and after, they tore around the house and yard, a hundred different things catching their attention every minute. At one point, Michael stood on the kitchen table and jumped in the butter dish, yelling, while Aaron flashed me that innocent, I'm-too-cute-for-my-own-good smile and then disappeared out the door.

I am amazed that there was nothing permanently damaged at the Stevensons' house. I'm an experienced baby-sitter who can usually control the kids I sit for. But on this night I was most definitely not in control.

Finally, it was bedtime, though it took me way longer than it should have to get the boys ready for bed. I wrestled their pajamas on, helped them brush their teeth, made sure they went to the bathroom, and got them countless just-one-more drinks of water. By the time they were settled into bed, it was already forty-five minutes past their official bedtime.

As I turned to leave the bedroom, one of them asked me to read a quick story to them. I was tempted to explain in a harsh tone that if they'd gotten ready for bed quicker, then they would have gotten a story. But something stopped me short. I looked at them both, now quietly tucked in their beds, and I saw a little of what their mother probably sees—not little terrors, but little boys who were just being boys with a new baby-sitter.

With one boy on either side of me, I started reading *The Little Engine That Could,* an obviously much-loved book. When I was done they mumbled drowsy thank-yous, but I could tell something was bothering Aaron. His confidence and charm were gone, and when I asked what was wrong, his lip started trembling and two full tears rolled down his cheek. "I miss my mommy," he said mournfully.

"I'm so sorry," I said. "I understand." I tucked him into bed with his favorite ragged blanket and tried to comfort him. I rubbed his back like "mommy does every night," and he soon relaxed.

I tiptoed out and right before I closed the door, he whispered, "Good night."

"Good night," I whispered and then walked out.

As I waited downstairs for their parents to come home, I felt a sweet sense of satisfaction. And it occurred to me how much we all are like those little boys with God. Some days we act like terrors. We sin and fail and make mistakes. But when we are finally tired out and feeling alone in the dark, we miss our Father. And thankfully our Father sees us the way I finally saw those boys—vulnerable, forgivable, and utterly lovable.

That reminder was worth much, even a wild night of baby-sitting.

As a bridegroom rejoices over his bride,
so will your God rejoice over you.
ISAIAH 62:5

I'm Pretty As a Princess

All little girls need to feel pretty. It begins when we're toddlers as people smile at us and say, "You look so pretty!" Right away we understand that "pretty" must be a good thing and that it pleases others. Soon enough we learn that pretty has to do with what we see in the mirror, what we look like.

As we move through our grade-school years, we decide just how pretty we are, based mostly on male feedback. When girls are little, affirmation that they're pretty comes (or should come) from dads, grandpas, and uncles. But as we grow up, the need shifts from wanting Daddy to think we're pretty to wanting guys our age to agree.

Now that I'm in high school, I see so many girls who are desperate to feel prettier. Some of them spend hours shopping, doing their makeup, brushing their hair, primping, curling, and dyeing. But in most cases, no matter how much they try, they still never feel pretty enough. How *can* they when they're surrounded by images of unattainable beauty in magazines and movies, where every imperfection has been digitally erased?

As long as we uphold these images as the definition of *pretty,* we'll always be insecure about how we look. In my case, for example, my stomach isn't flat enough, my eyes are too boring, my thighs are too fat…the list goes on.

You may be thinking, *But it's being pretty on the inside that matters most!*

We've all heard that said many times. But it's not much of a consolation, when in so many arenas of life, people don't act like what's inside is where it counts. Do the guys go for the girls who aren't pretty on the outside but who are pretty on the inside? Not very often. When girls are competing among themselves, is it over who is the kindest or has the sweetest disposition? Not very often. Usually it's over who has the prettiest hair or the most fashionable clothes.

But the real tragedy isn't so much that we care about what's outside, but that so often we associate being pretty with feeling *loved.* When someone tells us we're beautiful, we hear, "You're worthwhile, you're valuable, you're lovable!" And since we're not always going to be told we're pretty, that means many girls go around feeling unloved.

We all have to decide how we are going to respond to our

need to feel pretty. We can choose to get so caught up with how we look that we can't see anything else. We can keep on equating feeling pretty with feeling loved. We can get bitter about the whole thing and choose to pretend we don't care a bit about being pretty and let those around us know it.

Or we can admit that we *want* to feel pretty but understand that it's not the most important thing in life—and that it doesn't really bring us love. Pretty might get us a date on a Friday night, garner us admiring glances, or even improve our chances of attending a school dance. But prettiness has little to do with real love.

In the end, the only answer that makes sense is to think of our prettiness in terms of what God thinks of us rather than what the world thinks. Because it's not what's on the inside that counts, but rather Who is living inside. If God is living in your heart, He is just waiting to take you in His arms and whisper in your ear, "You are so pretty. I love you. I've made you, and you are so beautiful to Me."

Hearing those words and knowing the One who spoke them means it with all His heart should make you feel pretty as a princess. Because that is what you are.

If you race merely for the tributes from others, you will be at the mercy of their expectations.

Scott Tinley

Jesus Christ is the same yesterday and today and forever.
HEBREWS 13:8

Change Is Inevitable, but God Is Unchanging

There is a saying that's common where I live, and it goes like this: "The only thing predictable about Central Oregon weather is that it will be unpredictable."

Our lives are like that, aren't they? Predictably unpredictable. None of us really knows for sure what will happen next because change is inevitable.

If you're like me, that word *inevitable* can make you wary. It signifies that nothing can be done to prevent something from happening. That means if something is inevitable, we're not in control (and we all long to be in control!). When you pair *inevitable* with the word *change*, it conjures up feelings of powerlessness and even dread.

Life is full of changes that catch us off guard. A late-night phone call informing you of a terrible accident, a sudden announcement that your family will be moving to another state, a notice that you were not accepted to the college you planned to attend—such changes can throw our lives into panic mode.

Would life be easier if it were a nice, predictable flow of events? Definitely, yes. But if there were no surprises or changes, I think we would quickly find our lives boring. Even a person like me, who doesn't particularly like change, realizes that without it life would feel flat. We would all be like robots, just going through the motions.

Tonight I was on the phone with a friend who was in a car accident this past weekend. His car is totaled, and it is incredible that he is alive. He said something that stuck with me: "It's amazing how much God is in control. I was not in control at all in that car; it was all Him."

And that is so true. God knows what will happen to each and every one of us, and He is *completely* in control of it all. He will be with us through every imaginable and unimaginable surprise or turn our lives take. And because God *doesn't* change, we don't have to be afraid of the changes we face. When the winds of life become more unpredictable than usual and we feel tossed and blown about, we can always cling to the Rock who never moves or changes.

Knowing this makes the word *inevitable* seem a little less ominous and the word *change* maybe even a little exciting.

Never be afraid to trust

an unknown future

to a known God.

Corrie ten Boom

> Love the LORD your God with all your heart
> and with all your soul and with all your strength.
>
> DEUTERONOMY 6:5

I Don't Want to Be Religious

A couple of weeks ago I was at church for Wednesday-night youth group, and as people were up front talking and sharing honestly, I realized how much of a hypocrite I am. To any observer (even someone who knows me well), it would appear that I have everything in order. My life, my actions, and my words all look right and sound good; but in being totally honest with myself, I realized that what was going on inside me wasn't always matching outside appearances. When I was singing, I was worrying more about what the guy next to me thought than what God thought. And reading the Bible had become something I did to be a "good Christian" rather than to know God more.

The thing that sets Christianity apart from other religions is that Jesus doesn't want to change just our actions—He wants to change our hearts. And that night, all was not well in my heart.

Anything I do or don't do that looks good to everyone else means nothing to God if it isn't a result of my love for Him and doesn't come from my heart.

Personally, I don't have any desire to be "religious," follow a list of rules, or "do" Christianity. I don't want to be a hypocrite—alive and flourishing on the outside, but sick and withering inside.

So my recent prayer is that anything and everything I do for God would be a natural, unstoppable thing that flows straight from my heart and my love for Him. I want my love for my Jesus to be what gives me strength, to be my reason for getting up each day. And I believe this is what God wants more than anything, too.

He longs for us to serve Him because of our true, deep love for Him. He longs to change our hearts and, ultimately, our lives.

> Christianity in its purest form is nothing more than seeing Jesus. Christian service in its purest form is nothing more than imitating Him who we see. To see His majesty and to imitate Him, that is the sum of Christianity.
>
> Max Lucado

I thank my God every time
I remember you.

PHILIPPIANS 1:3

Memories Are a Treasure

I remember that winter. The snow was piled high, and the sky was an enveloping gray shroud. Every morning and afternoon the animals' water had to be broken, and at times the cold seemed unbearable. I think I was ten.

It was a dark, cold Saturday when we drove the five miles to our friends' neighborhood. Light, fluffy snowflakes were gently floating down, wetting our hair and faces. We weren't the only ones there that day; three or four other families joined us at the top of the hill. We parked the cars off the road and kids piled out, bundled in many-colored layers of manufactured warmth. In their arms were sleds of every kind—flying saucers, toboggans, inner tubes, sleds with brakes, sleds without brakes, and sleds with steering wheels.

We all congregated at the top of the hill and received the usual parental instructions: "Don't go too fast!" "Watch out for cars!" "Don't hit any trees!"—that sort of thing. Then we were off. Childlike screams filled the frigid air as our sleds picked up speed. We held onto our sleds, willing them to go farther and faster, for the one who went the farthest won.

When my sled finally came to a stop, I jumped off, grabbed the string attached to it, and started the long trek back up the hill. This routine was repeated again and again. (Occasionally I was able to convince one of the dads to carry my sled up the hill.)

I raced the boys and won most of the time, but one had a very fast sled that he wouldn't let anybody else use; he became the one to beat. Another of my friends had a thin, flexible mat that you rode on your stomach. He gave me a push, and I was off. All the others were walking up the hill or waiting their turn, so I was alone on the hill. Faster and faster I flew, the wind beating my face. As the slope evened out, I didn't slow down where I had before. I kept going, gliding easily past the mark of the previous record holder.

But all good things must come to an end, and I finally slowed to a stop. The others were too far away to be heard and silence was everywhere. I let out a loud "Woohoo!" before again trudging up the hill. My sled dragging behind me, I watched several of my fellow sledders whip by.

By the time I reached the top, I was so exhausted that I just lay down in the snow and stared up at the sky. The snow began falling harder, and it seemed like the sky was spitting snowflakes at me. A bundled-up face appeared over me, blocking the snowfall. "Time to go," my dad said, and he reached out his hand to pull me up.

The hill quickly emptied as sleds were thrown in the backs of cars and kids piled in. Our caravan of cars made its way slowly down the hill to our friends' house. We had only a few minutes to warm up before my parents wanted to go home. In a hurry to play with the other children, I gulped my hot chocolate, burning my mouth. I started crying, and several moms gathered around, trying to comfort me.

Before long, my family was loaded into our Suburban. My dad carried me to the car, as I was still crying about my burned tongue. Then we snuggled under blankets for the five-mile drive home.

I have such vivid memories of that day. I wouldn't change any of it if I could—not even the part with the hot chocolate. Those friends have since moved to another state, and I haven't seen them in a few years. Life has led us down different paths and presented us with different challenges. If and when I see them in the future, we all will have changed. But I will always have that memory, and it is something to be treasured.

When I was little I thought, I would marry that little boy

who let me borrow his sled. But I haven't seen him since we were twelve, and I wonder if when I see him again I'll know him at all. That is why I must treasure the memories I do have of him and of the rest of my life. Memories should never be let go, because they let us relive moments in our lives. Sometimes photographs and videotape don't do a scene justice, and the only thing powerful enough to capture the moment is our memory.

There are moments—things I have heard, things I have seen—that have stuck with me for years. As a child, I remember an adult telling me not to hold my breath because I was killing the little good guys in my brain. Every time I hold my breath now I think about that. I remember shopping for a prom dress with my mom, grandma, sister, and a friend just a little while ago. I remember asking Jesus into my heart when I was four, and how I felt when I told my dad. I remember my knee surgery and being awake afterward but not being able to open my eyes for about an hour. I remember learning to water-ski on my eighth birthday and getting an American Girl doll because of it. And I remember the day our friends moved away…

What do you remember?

Every moment that passes, good or bad, becomes a piece of who I am. These pieces, if not treasured, guarded, and held onto, could slip away. When I am old and gray, the memories I have stored will keep me company as much as anything else.

I have learned that the real treasures in life aren't just in the doing and living of them, but in remembering and retelling the important parts, the precious parts, over and over again.

For memory has painted

this perfect day

with colors that never fade.

Carrie Jacobs Bond

So God created man in his own image,
in the image of God he created him;
male and female he created them.

GENESIS 1:27

People Are More Alike than Different

I confess that I used to be a little afraid of people who seemed different from me. Growing up, I could easily talk with other people who were basketball fans, liked romantic movies, enjoyed being outdoors, or loved books. But when I encountered someone whose interests or culture or dress was completely foreign to me, I had a hard time talking with that person. It seemed we had nothing in common and, therefore, nothing to talk about. I immediately became uncomfortable and eventually tried to avoid conversations with such people.

But then I did something that I wish every young person could do: I traveled. And everywhere I went, whether to another state or another country, I learned more about how different—and how very much alike—we all really are.

The differences were most noticeable in foreign countries. The food was different (sometimes to the point that it was indescribable), as was the language, the culture, and the manner of dress. I was always a little cautious at first. But without fail, by the end of every trip, I always ended up wanting to stay.

Now, whether I'm visiting a "strange" place for a day or a couple of weeks, it's never long enough. I want to live there for a few months and really get to know the people and their culture on a personal level. I always feel a connection with the people, even if their lifestyle is strange to me. For example, even though my only communication with an old woman in Africa was a smile, I know she understood me. And although *hello* and *thank you* were the only words I could say in the little Latvian girl's language, we became inseparable friends while I was there.

My travels are a healthy reminder to me that no matter how different a person seems, God made every one of us in His image, so we're alike where it counts. It doesn't matter what we do for a living, where we live, which languages we speak, what we like to do, or what kinds of foods we eat. We all still fall in love, have secret hopes, get misunderstood, find jobs, celebrate holidays, cry from pain (whether physical or of the heart), and laugh with loved ones.

These things will always look different, particularly from the outside, from culture to culture and person to person. But I'm convinced that if we look deep into the heart of any human, we will all see someone familiar looking back at us. We will all recognize a little of ourselves.

> "The eye is the lamp of the body."
>
> MATTHEW 6:22

We Hear Best with Our Eyes

I always thought my parents told me to look at people when I talked to them because it was the polite thing to do. And it is. But it is so much more.

Personally, I find it hard to look people in the eyes for more than a second or two. One of my friends is especially gifted at this. She will talk to someone for less than a minute and then walk away and say to me, "Wow! She had the prettiest green eyes." I can ask her what color one of our friend's eyes are and she will be able to tell me immediately, without fail. This is because she makes and holds eye contact with people she talks to. What a wonderful habit!

The truth is, I couldn't tell you the color of any of my friends' eyes. I have to make a conscious effort to look people in the eyes, and although I've been getting a little better lately, I know I don't do it nearly often enough.

Yet when I talk to others, I appreciate it so much when they look me in the eyes. I feel like they value me and really care about what I'm saying. I feel respected, and it's so different from the feeling I get when I talk to someone who doesn't look at me. Because I appreciate it so much when others do it, I now make an effort to look people in the eyes, because I know it says that I am listening, that I care, and that they matter.

Like so many other instances in life, it is the little things that communicate so much. Remember this the next time you're talking with someone. If you really want to hear past his or her words and into his or her heart, don't just listen with your ears—listen with your eyes.

Every day we are called
to do small things
with great love.

Mother Teresa

> The purposes of a man's heart are deep waters,
> but a man of understanding draws them out.
>
> PROVERBS 20:5

My Mom Understands

When I was in junior high, I was utterly rejected by two of my very best friends. Maybe that doesn't sound all that traumatic. I know it happens all the time, but it was one of the hardest things that had happened to me in my first twelve years of life.

The three of us had been the best of friends, but then one day they decided just to be friends without me. I tried to be brave and pretend it wasn't a big deal. But as I sat on my couch watching them riding their bikes past my house, I started to cry. At first I tried to hold it in because I didn't think my mom would understand, and I wasn't sure I wanted to talk about it with her.

But my mom noticed something was wrong. She came over, sat down on the couch, and held me until I was ready to hear her. Then, with tears in her own eyes at the painful memory, she told me a story about when something similar had happened to her. The circumstances were not exactly the same, but I could tell that she knew what I was feeling. Knowing that someone else had gotten through it meant a lot to me, regardless of the fact that she is my mother.

Since that day in junior high, I cannot count the times when I've felt a certain way or was going through something difficult or overwhelming, and my mom was the friend who was there for me. When I came home from school angry over an argument with a friend, my mom let me express my frustration. When a boy asked me out for the first time, my mom gave me advice on what to do and how to respond. When I was trying to figure out what I really believed about God and why, my mom listened as I searched, questioned, and grew.

While I used to believe that adults couldn't relate because of the "impossible" differences between our generation and theirs, my mom has shown me that this is not always true. And the fact that it was my mom who showed me this makes it even more special. I have not only learned that she really understands, but I discovered in the process that she's become one of my dearest friends.

If you're like most people, you probably have grandparents or know elderly people who say, "When I was your age…" or "I remember when…," and a lot of the time you find it hard to relate to them. They seem so far away, like they can't understand because everything was so different for them. But the older you get, the more experiences and *potential* wisdom you gain. (I've also learned that not everyone who is older is wiser.)

So before you disregard adults, try really listening to what they have to say. Your mom or dad may not always understand, but more often than not they (or another adult you know) have experienced the same difficult feelings and tough situations. Talk to them and tell them how it really is with you. You might be surprised to discover that it's been that same way with them, too. And your parents just might become two of your closest friends.

For God, who said, "Let light shine out of darkness," made his light shine in our hearts to give us the light of the knowledge of the glory of God in the face of Christ.

2 CORINTHIANS 4:6

The Stars Shine Brighter When There Is No Moon

One of the benefits of living in a small town in Central Oregon is that the sky is very dark at night, unobscured by city lights. In other words, it's perfect for stargazing. On warm summer evenings, I sometimes lie on a blanket in our backyard and gaze at an indescribable masterpiece. Together the moon and the stars make a splendid picture, silent guardians over many a lovers' rendezvous and dreamer's wish.

However, the best time for stargazing is when the moon steps aside and lets the stars have center stage. Though gloriously beautiful in its own right, especially when it's full, the moon steals some of the magnificence of the stars. They appear to shine less brightly, their brilliant twinkling dulled by the lunar glow. But on black, moonless nights, the effect is glorious, as if someone shattered a crystal vase and scattered the pieces across the sky.

Now and then, shooting stars will dive across the sky. I think of them as overly exuberant stars that don't know what else to do with their brilliance but paint the sky with it. It's almost as if they suddenly realized that nothing is holding them back but themselves.

In many ways, the sky is like our world and the stars like people. We are all unique and special, numbered by God. We are His stars, created to shine brightly in His world. We are all given the chance to sparkle and shine in life.

But don't we all long to live like shooting stars? Don't we secretly wish we were basketball stars, talented artists, skiers destined for Olympic gold? The fact is that many of us often wonder if anyone really notices us in the vast universe. That's especially true when a "moon" is near. Moons are those people who make us feel that we are fading into the background. Sometimes they even seem to force us there.

When these "moons" are in the room, we imagine that we simply disappear. We feel overwhelmed or outclassed by these people, our confidence shrinks, and we're pretty sure our own little light has dimmed to a mere flicker.

But you know what? The stars don't *really* shine any less brightly when the moon is out. From where we lie, gazing up at the sky, the stars only *seem* to have dulled. But in reality, every star is still shining with exactly the same intensity as on a moonless night.

It is God who always sees us when we shine, no matter how big and bright the moons around us. The Ultimate Stargazer has given each of us the ability to shine, and He has created the perfect plan and time for us to do so. But unlike the stars, it's up to us how brightly we want our light to shine. Will we be shooting stars, so alive and exuberant that we just have to show the world our joy? Or will we be like those distant stars that flicker and fade, so that one second you see them and the next you don't?

Imagine you are lying beside me, watching the sky clustered with brilliant stars. No words are necessary. There is nothing to say, but at the same time we want to say so much. We gaze in silent awe, gasping when the occasional shooting star hurtles its brilliance across the sky, like a special person making his mark in the world. Will that be me someday? Will it be you?

It can. All we have to do is claim our intended place in God's universe, let our lights shine brightly, and then smile at the world as we soar by.

Shoot for the moon because if you miss, you'll land among the stars.

Les Brown

Pedestals Weren't Made for People

Ashlee was my idol. I wanted to be just like her when I grew up. I longed to wear the same clothes, laugh the same way, and do the same things as she. We were friends, but she was definitely the leader in the friendship. Whatever she thought we should do always sounded great to me. I was so proud of Ashlee, proud that she called me her friend. Others told me that I shouldn't spend so much time with her, that I let her control me and make decisions for me. But I didn't hear them, because in my mind Ashlee could do no wrong.

Eventually I began to see what everyone else had been telling me all along. I slowly began to see that Ashlee was really very selfish, demanding, and dishonest. She tried to take advantage of other people, and she really didn't care about the consequences. I realized that she was not the angel that I always imagined her to be; she was actually a very unhappy person. It was devastating to me when I first realized this. Ashlee was in fact very real and very human and not the kind of person I wanted to model my life after.

I can recall so many times when the people I know and love have made mistakes or let me down. The better you know someone, the more clearly you see his or her faults. His or her shortcomings become glaringly obvious to you, sometimes to the point where it seems like he or she is doing those things on purpose.

I don't know how many Ashlees I've known in my life. I know they're not perfect, but sometimes it's hard to believe that they are capable of making mistakes (at least, not any big ones). But without fail, each of those people that I've put on a pedestal (either outwardly or subconsciously) has completely messed up in some way, quickly reminding me that nobody is perfect.

It's not bad to admire, respect, and want to be like someone, whether our role model is a famous athlete, an artist, a pastor, or a friend. It's when we idealize (or idolize) a person that things get a little messed up. Sooner or later he or she will do something that disappoints us. We might feel hurt and even betrayed. But it's our own fault, because we had unrealistic expectations of that person.

In our lives there will always be Ashlees that we believe to be perfect, or at least closer to perfect than the rest of us. It can be hard not to idolize someone who seems to have it all together. But next time you catch yourself putting someone on a pedestal, remember that no one can hold up under the weight of your expectations.

☆ ----- ☆

> A cheerful look brings joy to the heart.
>
> PROVERBS 15:30

Children Know the Secret of Making Friends

During my childhood years, my parents often invited to dinner families that we kids didn't know very well. When the guests were adults only, my siblings and I knew it would be an easy night. After dinner and dessert we would go up to our rooms or outside to play. But when kids were going to be among our guests, my mom would always remind us that it was our responsibility to demonstrate hospitality, to make them feel welcome in our home.

After the introductions of our guests and their children, it was always very quiet and uncomfortable for a few minutes. My sister would show them her room, and then my brother would show them his animals. Then we tried to make conversation. "Do you like basketball?" and "How old are you?" were typical questions.

We usually got a sentence or less in response. Very quickly, we would run out of things to talk about, and we would all sit there in silence, smiling nervously. After a couple of awkward minutes, someone, usually my brother, would suggest something fun to do—basketball, hide-and-seek, ghosts-in-the-graveyard, and tag were among our favorite diversions.

As we played, a funny thing began to happen. We would start laughing and joking with each other, and before long we were all "buds." When my mom called us inside or downstairs, we would race to the kitchen, breathless and smiling. The rest of the evening flew by, and when the adults were ready to go, we hugged our new friends good-bye, with promises to write or call, depending on the situation.

It still amazes me how those evenings suddenly changed when we started having fun together. During a basketball game or a competitive game of tag, we forgot about our shyness or the fact that we hardly knew each other. And in the process, we became friends. In fact, some of those friendships that started with a simple game of hide-and-seek are still among my most treasured.

I don't think my experience is unique. If you watch young kids trying to get acquainted with other kids, you quickly realize that they know a secret that the rest of us sometimes forget: Having fun with someone opens the door for friendship.

It doesn't matters who you are or how old you are. If you

want to offer your friendship to someone, do something fun together. Maybe go bowling, putt-putt golfing, or rafting. Maybe plan a picnic and a bike ride with a silly destination. Or maybe play a game of hide-and-seek at the park. The activity you choose is not important. What matters is that you relax, laugh, and let the fun-loving child inside of you come out to play.

Be glad of life,

for it gives you a chance to work,

play and look at the stars.

Henry Van Dyke

"The LORD does not look at the things man looks at. Man looks at the outward appearance, but the LORD looks at the heart."

1 SAMUEL 16:7

Stereotypes Are Shortcuts

E very day in school, I see people being categorized and labeled according to appearance. Making assumptions about people based on what they wear or how they look is wrong and sad. But I have to admit that I have often done it myself. It's just easier when you meet someone new to place him or her in a recognizable category or group. It's like taking a shortcut in the process of getting to know a person.

More often than not, I've come to discover that my stereotypes were off the mark. Sure, there are times when you can tell a jock is a jock or a skater is a skater just by looking at him. But most of the time you can't do this reliably. Maybe that guy I assumed was a skater who cared nothing about school is really a genius at science. Or the girl I checked off as a ditzy cheerleader, maybe she really would understand me as much as my best friend does.

Maybe the guy I thought was a jock is happy being a jock. And even if that's true, he's still *more* than a jock. I'm learning that no person, no matter how much he or she seems to fit within a narrowly defined group, has only the characteristics or interests we typically associate with that particular group.

I used to think it was wrong to stereotype people simply because it wasn't fair to them. But recently it has become clear to me that when I do this, I'm also not being fair to *myself.* How many friends, surprises, and joys have I missed out on because I assumed more than I asked about someone, or because I encountered a person's appearance but missed his heart?

It's hard to change old habits, ways of reacting to people that are ingrained in you. But I'm ready to throw out those neat little boxes people never really fit in anyway. There's so much more to every person we meet, no matter how neatly they seem to fit our preconceived notions.

Instead of taking shortcuts and making assumptions, take the time to really get to know someone. Only then will you discover what amazing, unique, and incredible people God has decided to put in your path.

> Whoever does not love
> does not know God,
> because God is love.
>
> 1 JOHN 4:8

Love Has a Name

The need to be loved is a deeply felt need ingrained in every person. From little babies who need to be held close, to the middle-class husband who needs a word of encouragement and a smile from his wife, to the eighty-year-old grandma who wants someone—anyone—to ask, "How are you?" and not mean just physically. All of us, no matter what or who we are, are looking for love.

But many people fail to find love—*real* love—because they are looking in the wrong places. The places they search may promise love and acceptance, but in reality offer only pain and rejection. I think of my many friends who fit this description, and it makes me sad. A lot of the girls I know are searching so hard for love from the opposite sex, whether from boyfriends or just guys in general. They put all of their hearts into their romantic relationships. But I know from just watching them that they're still not satisfied. Their lives are lacking deep, soul-satisfying love.

Then there are those people who seek love and seem to find it, but still it's not enough. I am convinced that a friend of mine is anorexic. She strives so hard after love and acceptance that she is willing to starve herself, hoping an attractive figure will bring her the love she so desperately needs. What tears me up is that she *is* loved already but just doesn't see it. So many people value and love her for the person she is, not just for her beauty. Yet she still continues her search for love, and in the process she is literally killing herself.

I believe the reason she doesn't see that all these people love her is that she has never experienced the love of God. She doesn't realize that love has a name, and it is God. No matter where we search or what type of love we think we're looking for, God is the best and most perfect Lover. This is true not just because He loves us, but because He *is* love. And it's only when we experience His love that we are able to recognize and receive love when it comes to us in human form. Only after we have drunk from the source of love Himself can we really give and receive the kind of love that will never fail to satisfy.

In the end, there is only one right place to look for love, and that's within the arms of one who is Himself love.

The One who loves you most
can do anything—except
He cannot love you more.

James Langteaux

We Should Work at Liking Work

I was sitting on the couch, watching some movie I'd seen too many times already. I needed to get up and shovel out the horse manure in the stalls, but I had no motivation to go do it. I kept thinking how much I didn't want to go outside and do my chores when I suddenly thought of a book I had been reading. The story was set in America in the 1800s, and the characters (including the teenagers) not only worked hard, but also *valued* work.

How different that is from the way things are today! We've gone from a country founded on the Puritan work ethic to a country that nearly despises work. Work is no longer considered a calling or even a responsibility but, rather, an evil that must be endured so that we might fully enjoy life during our leisure time. Most people with jobs count the weeks until their next vacation, keeping one eye on the clock at all times. They live for the weekends, but wake up Sunday dreading the coming Monday.

I think this mind-set is a sad one, one that can't be good for our country.

I am not trying to say that we should always get excited about work or that it's the most important thing in life. But a large portion of our waking hours is made up of work, whether we like it or not. And so it seems to me that one key to a happy life is learning to enjoy work, whether we're working with our hands or at a desk or whatever.

Here's another problem with how we view work: Unlike the old days when work was valued for itself, now its value is usually measured by money. As a result, many people take jobs that pay well, but they end up dissatisfied and working halfheartedly. Some of them may be considered very successful, but they hate their jobs or work too many hours at the expense of their families.

That's not what I want; I don't think there are many of us who want that. If we're going to spend a good portion of our lives working, we need to learn to enjoy it. We need to choose careers based not only on money but also on how the work fulfills us and how it affects the people we love.

In order to do that, I think we need some major "attitude adjustments," as my mom calls them. The first is to get over our repulsion toward work. The second is to make sure the line of work we pursue doesn't repulse us!

After thinking about these things, I was finally able to stop my movie and head outside to the barn. And you know what? Shoveling the manure wasn't so bad. I sang summer-camp songs exuberantly while I worked because no one was around. I found myself laughing and even really enjoying myself.

But I did decide that I will definitely *not* make shoveling manure my life's work.

> Bear with each other and forgive whatever grievances you
> may have against one another. Forgive as the Lord forgave you.
>
> COLOSSIANS 3:13

Three Little Words Can Set You Free

S orry, Danae." He sounded sincerely sad, but I stared straight ahead, not wanting to risk catching his eye. Those two words seemed so small and insignificant compared to the hurt he had dealt me over the past couple of weeks. As we sat in silence, voices of people walking past my car faded in and out, but it was like they were part of a different world.

"Please?" he said again. "I am so sorry." A part of me softened, wanting to hug him and tell him I would forgive him; but then my stomach twisted as I remembered how he'd lied to me and ignored me, his best friend.

I swallowed hard and said nothing.

I know this story might make it sound like I'm not a very forgiving person, but the truth is that I'm usually pretty quick to forgive. I'll forgive my close friend when she goes to sleep instead of calling me back. I'll forgive my brother for borrowing my CDs without permission and then returning them scratched. I'll even forgive my mom for telling someone I'll baby-sit without checking with me first.

But I'm discovering that it's much harder to forgive people when they hurt me in a personal way, a way that cuts right to the heart. When my good friend ignores me because of all his new friends, for example. Or when a friend says bad things about me to someone else and then lies to me about it. I know that I should forgive these people, especially because I love them, but it's never that easy.

I think these kinds of deep hurts happen in high school more than anywhere else. The quest to achieve popularity is such a huge part of life that often friendships get mangled or sacrificed in the process. It's kind of ironic. We all want to feel accepted and liked by as many people as possible, but sometimes, in trying to achieve this, we cause people we care about to feel just the opposite.

As I sat there with my friend, trying to hold back tears, I knew I needed to forgive him. Not just for his sake, but for mine, too. My tears weren't all I was holding inside. I was also holding onto bitterness, and that hurt almost as much as what my friend had done in the first place.

When you're the one being hurt, it seems too easy for the other person to simply say "I'm sorry." And everything is supposed to be forgiven and forgotten, just like that! It's not fair, no matter how you look at it.

But as I considered this, it suddenly hit me that this was exactly what Jesus did for me. How could I not forgive my friend when Jesus has forgiven me for everything when I least deserved it? How could I withhold forgiveness when every single day He forgives me for so much more than what my friend was asking?

Finally I looked my friend in the eye and told him that I forgave him. I felt a huge relief, as my heart slowly emptied of all the hurt I'd been carrying around. Everything between my friend and me felt fresh and new and right again. We were both set free.

And all it took was three little words: *I forgive you.*

When I was a child, I talked like a child, I thought like a child,
I reasoned like a child. When I became a man,
I put childish ways behind me. And now these three remain:
faith, hope and love. But the greatest of these is love.

1 CORINTHIANS 13:11, 13

I'll Never Be Too Big
for Hugs

When I was a little girl, I dreaded the thought of growing up. I remember sobbing to my mom that I wanted to stay the same age and never get any older. Mom gently told me that all children must grow up. And then she told me of all the wonderful things I would never be able to do if I didn't, things like driving a car, going to movies with my friends, falling in love, and staying up all night.

Her reasoning did not convince me immediately, but a few years later the lesson apparently sank in. When I was in junior high, I couldn't *wait* to get older. And it was about that time I adopted the typical I-don't-want-to-be-too-closely-associated-with-my-parents attitude. I remember my mom dropping me off somewhere, and as I got out of the car I thought that I should probably hug her. But instead of throwing my arms about her, I nonchalantly hopped out of the car and shut the door.

Hugging my parents had become a chore rather than an expression of love.

These days I can't wait to be done with high school, to go to college and experience a whole different world. But I'm also frightened. Sometimes the idea of leaving home makes me want to curl up in my mom's arms and sob like I used to, telling her that I don't want to grow up.

I wonder if how I'm feeling might actually be a good sign, or at least a normal stage. Maybe it's not until you come full circle, back to the point of treasuring your parents and not wanting to leave them, that you are finally, truly *ready* to leave. Maybe part of growing up is realizing that although you are no longer a child in age, you will always be your parents' child.

And you will never, ever be too big for hugs.

> O LORD, you have searched me and you know me.
> You know when I sit and when I rise;
> you perceive my thoughts from afar. You discern my going out
> and my lying down; you are familiar with all my ways.
>
> PSALM 139:1-3

The Hardest Person to Be Is Yourself

Last year I switched schools, and the change was harder than I thought it would be. At my old school, the classes were small and everybody knew everyone else really well; I had no problem being myself because we were all best friends.

The school I go to now is more than ten times the size of my previous school, and the atmosphere is entirely different. I have friends at my new school, but I've struggled with not being myself, and that has really bothered me.

From the first day at the new school I put on a mask. People would say, "How do you like it here?" or "How's your day going?" and no matter what the truth was, I always responded positively. I didn't feel like I could be real and honest with people. I was scared to be myself, even though I longed to show the real me.

Being yourself sounds simple, but for most of us, it's anything but.

We automatically erect invisible walls or put on "masks" that hide our true personalities and emotions when we're not sure we'll be accepted. For some people, this means withdrawing into their shells and being very shy and quiet. Others build protective walls by being very outgoing and loud, always the center of attention. And for others it's trying to act like someone else, someone they perceive to be more likable or acceptable.

I think more people than we know—or care to admit—go through life trying to be someone else, or only revealing a part of themselves.

One of the reasons this happens is that, to begin with, you have to figure out *who you are* before you can be yourself. For me, this has been a slow process, one that started long before I switched schools. It began with realizing that I had learned to gauge my identity by how others reacted to me and by what they expected of me. Clearly this was a problem. How could others tell me who I was on the inside, especially when I didn't let them see what's inside?

But if *I* didn't know who I was and *they* didn't either, then who did?

The answer was obvious: God. I had a choice: I could define who I am by looking at the world and believing the reflection of myself I saw there, or I could define myself by gazing at God (the only one who really knows me) and seeing myself as He sees me—just the way He made me.

Once you see yourself in light of how God sees you, then you begin to know who you *really* are, and you're ready for the next step: being yourself.

Sure, you will continue to face new situations and challenges that make you want to run to the closet and rummage around for your favorite mask. But once you see yourself as God sees you, you can begin to see those same situations as opportunities to let down your guard and *take off the mask.* Suddenly you can introduce yourself to someone new, have a meaningful conversation with someone you don't know very well, drop your protective walls, and let people see the real you.

As I slowly let down my walls and tried to be real at school, amazing things started happening. I met so many new, incredible people. I connected with and became much closer to people who had been casual friends, and I began having interesting conversations with people about things that really mattered.

And you know what? I discovered that the best way to help others let down *their* guards and take off *their own* masks was to take off mine. The more I was determined to be the real me, the more other people became real with me.

No matter how nervous or scared you are to be yourself, I hope you will learn to permanently take off your mask. It's tough, I know, but it's worth it. And not just for you, but also for everyone who is lucky enough to meet and really get to know the real you.

> **People are lonely because they build walls instead of bridges.**
>
> Aristotle

☆-----☆

You Can't Get Close to Someone without Taking Risks

This evening I went out to the barn, where our horses had already been fed. When I flipped on the lights, one of the horses poked his head out over his gate. I could tell that he'd been asleep because he kept blinking his eyes, trying to adjust to the light. He nickered and I walked over to pet him. The look in his eyes left no doubt in my mind that he trusts me implicitly.

Knowing a person trusts you is a gift. But knowing that a powerful animal descended from wild beasts trusts you is something so special that you cannot understand it unless you've experienced it. Most people don't realize that when a horse allows a human to pick up his hoof, this is a huge step of trust for the horse. Its primary means of defense is its legs. Horses are flight animals—they run from trouble. By letting a human pick up their hoof, they are giving up their instinctive means of escape.

People are a lot like horses this way. Sometimes we find it hard to trust even friends we love. After all, every time we accept a friend's help, lean on him or her, or confide a deep personal secret, it's as if we are handing them our foot—we are putting ourselves in a vulnerable position where we could be taken advantage of or easily hurt.

No wonder we so often choose to put up barriers, keep our conversations on a surface level, and run away from situations where we don't feel comfortable.

I know because I've done that so many times over the years.

But something that my horse knows well and I need to remember is that a little connection and affection are always worth waking up for. You can't get close to someone without taking a few risks. And when it comes to relationships, trusting someone with a piece of your heart is one of the best risks to take in life.

Life Is Short and Death Unthwartable

I *lost my wife and little boy. Someone crossed that yellow line…"*

I woke up this morning with those words from a song running through my head. I started thinking about what it would be like if I were killed in a car accident on the way to school.

I thought of certain friends and how they would respond when notified of my death. My thoughts shifted to the memorial service, to what people would say about me and my life. The image brought tears to my eyes as I wondered if my life would have mattered. I felt like George Bailey in *It's a Wonderful Life* as I thought of all the people whose lives I had somehow affected. Then I thought of all the people I *could* have influenced and all the opportunities I've let slip away.

The idea that life is short and death unthwartable was suddenly real to me.

I guess we all know that death is unavoidable, although adults are always saying that we teens think we're immortal. Maybe it's just that the full impact of death's inevitability hasn't really hit us. Only when something drastic happens do we stop running and realize how short life is. The fact is there in the back of our minds; but because we don't face death on a daily basis, we don't think much about it.

The reality is that when my life is finished, I can never go back and do it over—and that scares me. But like everyone else, I don't always act any different because of this knowledge.

On mornings like today, when I'm thinking about the shortness of my life, one thing becomes increasingly clear to me: *Love* is the only thing that's going to count when my life is over. *Have I loved others to the fullest?* I ask myself this question, and I wish the answer was always yes.

I know that I don't always love people to the fullest, because there is so much more to loving people than saying the words *I love you.*

As I sit here and think about life and death and the meaning of it all, many thoughts run through my head about what love is, if it truly is more than three words. So here goes.

Love is...

...asking about someone's day and truly caring about the answer.

...knowing that people are different and loving them just the same.

...being there.

...taking out the trash without being asked. ☺

...leaving the last pop for your brother, even though you've been craving it all day.

...being patient, even when you're tired—especially when you're tired.

...writing a note of encouragement.

...treating your family as well as you treat your friends.

...getting up early to do someone else's job for him.

...buying someone flowers for no reason.

...listening to your friend, even when you've heard the same thing a hundred times before.

...calling someone back after an argument.

...being honest about how you feel.

...caring—even when it's hard and you don't feel like it.

...trusting in someone even when you're scared.

...saying you're sorry when you are wrong.

...*listening and giving advice—and knowing the difference between the two.*

...*smiling in hard times.*

...*calling just to say hi on a busy day.*

...*praying for someone.*

...*forgiving someone again and again.*

...*walking beside someone, not in front of or behind her.*

...*believing.*

...*being comfortable with someone in silence.*

...*being a person to joke with.*

...*giving good hugs and long back rubs.*

...*providing a shoulder to cry on.*

...*being a friend.*

...*difficult.*

...*accepting people like a little child does.*

...*surprising someone.*

...*dying for someone.*

...*offering a new perspective on life.*

...*serving someone breakfast in bed.*

...*holding your tongue.*

...*not changing the radio station when someone is listening to it.*

...*gently admonishing.*

...*working on the things you know bother someone else.*

…trying to understand.
…sacrificial.
…being open to correction.
…ignoring another's faults.
…humble.
…serving others.
…changing your plans for someone.
…crying for someone when you know they're hurting.
…what God does to us.

There are many ways to say "I love you." In my family, "I love you's" are exchanged a number of times each day. I realize that saying it is important, and I'm glad that's how it is at home. But there is a difference between telling someone that you love them and telling them *why.* Life is short. If I'm on the phone with my dad and I don't tell him, "Dad, I love you for being my dad," I might not get another chance.

When people tell me why they love me, it puts a smile on my face for the rest of the day. Hearing something like that is encouraging, and it helps me remember that loving others is what really matters.

And yet there are many people in my life to whom I say "I love you" (and some not even that) without ever telling them *why* I love them. This is something I am going to change starting now, because life *is* short and death unthwartable. I want these people to know they are important to me.

I have learned that love is so much more than three little words. There's a song that goes something like "Love isn't someplace you fall—it's something you do." Love is a process that is learned. Not one person has mastered it, but it is the most important thing in this short life.

C. S. Lewis said, "[God] does not care how much we know, but how much we have loved." If death is unthwartable, then this statement puts life back into perspective. It's so easy to be distracted by school, work, stress, and our many responsibilities. But when it comes down to it, all that matters is how much we have loved.

Blessed is the influence
of one true, loving human soul
on another.

George Eliot

Run in such a way as to get the prize.
1 CORINTHIANS 9:24

Passionate People Get More out of Life

Passion. When I think of passion, I immediately think of two of my friends.

One is very competitive. No matter what we're playing, be it a card game or basketball, he plays to *win*. He puts almost as much heart and effort into our after-school pickup games as he did in the state tournament. That's just how he is made—no matter what the contest, he's going to give it his all. At times people have become upset with him because he gets so intense, whether we're playing in PE or just for fun. But I love that about him. I know he is having a blast. His philosophy is that if you're going to do something, you might as well try your hardest and give it your best.

The other friend I think of when I hear the word *passion* is a person who walks into a room and lights up the place. Her smile is infectious, and she loves to talk with people. She is very expressive, and whether she's acting the lead part in a play or simply explaining a homework assignment to you, she gets excited about it. Life to her is something to be treasured and lived wholeheartedly. If she is involved in something or believes in something, it commands all of her. There is no holding back; she gives everything.

I love being around these two people because their passion is inspiring and it flows through every aspect of their lives. Their love and commitment to giving all of themselves to what they do makes me want to live like that. They make me, as another friend of mine said, "not want to live an average life."

One of the worst things I can think of is to see someone half committed to something. If you're going to give yourself to something, like my friend who gets into sports, why not make it worth your time? Why not give your all to something that will last, something that matters, instead of giving only part of you to something that will not last? Life is too short to be lived halfheartedly and apathetically.

All my life I've wanted to be like that—so passionate about something that I just can't stop talking about it. This something that I long to have consume me, to take control of every part of me, is God. I want to be completely and passionately devoted to Him. I am far from where I long to be—daily I see things that are more important to me than Him. But I know that God is molding me into the person He wants me to be. God hasn't given up on me; He hasn't given up on anybody.

So instead of living halfheartedly, let's make this life worth living. Let's stand up for what we believe and not back down. Let's get carried away and throw our everything into life. After all, we have but one life to give—and one life to live.

I wish that life should not be cheap, but sacred.
I wish days to be as centuries,
loaded and fragrant.

Ralph Waldo Emerson

Multnomah Publishers

The publisher and author would love to hear your
comments about this book. *Please contact us at:*
www.multnomahbooks.net/thingslearned